UNFINISHED WAR

A Journey through Civil War in Yemen

Asmaa Waguih

HELION & COMPANY

To Riccardo

Helion & Company Limited
Unit 8 Amherst Business Centre
Budbrooke Road
Warwick
CV34 5WE
England
Tel. 01926 499 619
Email: info@helion.co.uk
Website: www.helion.co.uk
X (formerly Twitter): @helionbooks
Visit our blog https://helionbooks.wordpress.com/

Published by Helion & Company 2024
Designed and typeset by Paul Hewitt, Battlefield Design (www.battlefield-design.co.uk)
Cover designed by Paul Hewitt, Battlefield Design (www.battlefield-design.co.uk)

ISBN 978-1-804515-86-0

British Library Cataloguing-in-Publication Data.
A catalogue record for this book is available from the British Library.

For details of other titles published by Helion & Company Limited contact the above address or visit our website: http://www.helion.co.uk.

We always welcome receiving book proposals from prospective authors.

Acknowledgements

Thanks to: the people of Yemen who welcomed me, hosted and assisted me throughout my missions across their country; to Ricccardo Privitera, without whom this book would never have existed and for his creative work on the design of this book; to Mohammed Ghobari, for his continuous support in Yemen and his insightful editing of the Arabic text; to Marwa Awad, for her assistance with editing the English text; and to Zlatolin Donchev for his editorial ideas and insights.

These photographs were captured during the period between April 2016 and February 2022 and represent only the time of their taking. The text is based on my interviews with various Yemeni citizens, officials, journalists and researchers.

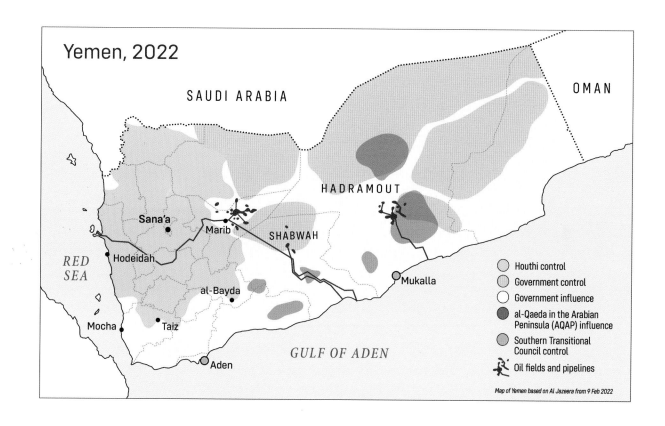

Yemen, 2022

SAUDI ARABIA

OMAN

HADRAMOUT

Sana'a

Marib

SHABWAH

RED SEA

Hodeidah

al-Bayda

Mukalla

Mocha

Taiz

GULF OF ADEN

Aden

- Houthi control
- Government control
- Government influence
- al-Qaeda in the Arabian Peninsula (AQAP) influence
- Southern Transitional Council control
- Oil fields and pipelines

Map of Yemen based on Al Jazeera from 9 Feb 2022

Contents

Foreword

From the bustling markets of Sana'a, the Yemeni capital, to the shores of Hodeida, the western port city that became a lifeline to all Houthi-controlled territories, to the ancient Throne of Bilqis in the eastern city of Marib, to the besieged city of Taiz, the cultural hub, and the fragmented south of Yemen, Asmaa Waguih takes readers on a visual tour deep in the country's dusty alleys that have witnessed repeated cycles of destruction and resilience in the past decade.

With its stunning images from across the country, Waguih's book tells the story of a forgotten war and its humanitarian crisis, without losing sight of Yemen's traditions, rich history, breathtaking landscape, its youth and elders, even in the most desperate places like a city under siege for nearly nine years.

Waguih is one of few journalists who have relentlessly travelled from the northern part of Yemen that shares borders with Saudi Arabia, to the south that overlooks the Arabian Sea, and from the western regions to the east, to get a fuller picture of a country at war.

Most of the media coverage in the past decade has opted to be selective in giving attention to the hallmarks of the Saudi-led coalition campaign in Yemen, instead of going deep into the root causes of the war, the history of each of the main players, the different parties' aspirations, tactics, finances, and weapons.

While many parties have committed crimes against civilians to varying degrees, most of the coverage has given an incomplete picture about Yemen's war, hoping to hold only one side accountable while giving a free pass to the others.

Saudi Arabia which led a campaign allegedly to dislodge the Houthis and restore the internationally-recognised government in Yemen has been implicated in a series of lethal attacks that amounted to war crimes. However, by giving little attention to the Houthis in most media coverage, the rebel group has enjoyed a free hand in committing atrocities, without much scrutiny or accountability, and continued to rule most of Yemen's population with an iron fist, imposing a dictatorial rule, while acting as an Iranian proxy when it comes to foreign policy.

Houthis are now attracting world-wide attention after waging a campaign against Israel-bound ships crossing the Arabian Sea, Bab-el-Mandab, and the Red Sea with volleys of missiles and drones allegedly as a way to punish Israel for its war in Gaza.

The attacks on the ships crossing the Red Sea brought counterattacks by the US and other Western countries, which had for a long time turned a blind eye to the Houthis' growing power and domination over the southern part of the Arabian Peninsula.

As the West is just waking up now to the Houthi threat, the book becomes of increasing importance as it draws readers closer to Yemen's people and landscape throughout the past decade.

The book is a visual documentation of Yemen's unfinished war.

Maggie Michael
Cairo-based journalist and Pulitzer Prize winner

Left: A billboard showing the late former-president Ali Abdullah Saleh hangs on the building of the central committee of the General People's Congress, Saleh's political party.

Timeline of Yemen's slide into conflict and war

1990 North and South Yemen unified to form a single state under President Ali Abdullah Saleh.

1994 In a civil war, Saleh prevents southern Yemen – angered by what it sees as its lower status – from splitting with northern Yemen.

2003 –2009 A Houthi group in northern Yemen protests marginalisation of the local Zaydi Shia Muslim sect, and fights six wars with Saleh's forces and one with Saudi Arabia.

2011 Arab Spring protests undermine Saleh's rule, leading to splits in the army and allow al-Qaeda in the Arabian Peninsula (AQAP) to seize territory in the east.

2012 Saleh steps down in a political transition plan backed by Gulf states. Abd-Rabbu Mansour Hadi becomes interim president and oversees a national dialogue to draft a more inclusive, federal constitution.

2013 -2014 AQAP stages attacks across Yemen. The Houthis seize the capital Sana'a in September 2014 with help from Saleh and demand a share of power.

2015 Hadi tries to announce a new federal constitution opposed by the Iran-aligned Houthis and Saleh, who arrest him. He escapes, pursued by the Houthis. Saudi Arabia, leading a coalition, intervenes in March, driving the Houthis and Saleh loyalists from Aden in south Yemen and from Marib, northeast of Sana'a. The front lines solidify, heralding years of deadlock.

2016 AQAP establishes a mini-state around Mukalla. The UAE backs local forces in a battle that ends AQAP rule there. Hunger grows as the coalition imposes a partial blockade on Yemen, claiming Iran is smuggling missiles to the Houthis, which Iran denies. Coalition air raids that kill civilians prompt warnings from human rights groups, but Western support for the military campaign continues.

2017 The Houthis fire a growing number of missiles deep into Saudi Arabia. Saleh switches sides but is killed trying to escape the Houthis.

2018 Coalition-backed forces advance up the Red Sea coast against the Houthis, aiming to take the port of Hodeidah, which handles the bulk of Yemen's commercial and aid imports. A military deadlock ensues. Peace talks are held in Sweden, the first in two years, and the warring sides agree to a truce and a troop withdrawal from Hodeidah. Work on a prisoner swap begins.

2019 The Hodeidah truce mostly holds but the withdrawal fails to materialise. Violence continues elsewhere. The UAE largely ends its presence, while still supporting local allies – Including southern separatists who seize Aden in August. Riyadh brokers a power-sharing deal between separatists and Hadi's government but implementation only begins in 2020.

2020 The Saudi-led coalition announces a truce prompted by COVID-19 but no progress is made to forge a permanent ceasefire and violence continues, although the warring sides do complete a prisoner swap. An attack on Aden airport moments after a plane lands carrying the newly formed power-sharing government kills at least 22 people. Riyadh and Hadi's government blame the Houthis.

2021 US President Joe Biden revokes the US "terrorist" designation placed on the Houthis, while also ending US support for offensive coalition operations. The Houthis intensify an offensive to seize gas-rich Marib, the government's last stronghold in northern Yemen. The UN and US envoys try to engineer a permanent truce and reopening of air and sea links to Houthi areas, but the warring sides resist compromise. Saudi Arabia and Iran launch direct talks, mostly focused on Yemen.

2022 Houthis extend missile and drone attacks to the UAE after Emirati-backed local militias battle the group in energy-producing Shabwa and Marib. Coalition warplanes pummel Yemen. The US acts to boost the military capabilities of Gulf allies amid strained relations and intensifying Houthi assaults on Saudi oil facilities. President Hadi cedes power to a presidential council in April as Riyadh acts to strengthen the anti-Houthi alliance. The warring parties agree a truce deal in April, which is rolled over twice and expires in October without an agreement to extend. But a tentative calm holds.

2023 In March, Saudi Arabia and Iran agree to restore relations, raising hopes that the Yemen peace process could see progress.

Preface

I was shot in Cairo on 14 August 2013. On that day Egyptian security forces stormed a sit-in of supporters of the ousted President Mohamed Morsi at the Rabaa Al-Adawiya Square with tear gas and live bullets. I was there as a photojournalist for Reuters when a shell from their wild firing ricocheted into my ankle.

I couldn't walk for almost seven months but while my injury has mostly healed the outcome for the more than 1,000 people reportedly killed in the Rabaa Massacre that day was irreversible (the figure is according to Human Rights Watch). The killings were a dark riposte to the optimism of the early days of the Arab Spring; an era of uprisings, civil wars and unsteady progress towards self-determination, that saw long-serving authoritarian rulers overthrown in early 2011 and hope of a better future emerge.

But if you ask the people of the region today what they think about the Arab Spring most will say they wish it had never happened.

The feeling of social inequality which fuelled the protests has deepened since 2010. This is most true in Yemen, Syria and Libya, countries which were shattered when street demonstrations morphed into civil wars and ultimately foreign interventions.

Of all those places I was most drawn to Yemen, a country which had been lodged in my consciousness since childhood. From my Cairo base, I covered the story of the Arab Spring for Reuters across the Middle East: in Egypt, Libya, and Syria, but somehow never Yemen.

My father's stories of his time serving as an Egyptian military officer, fighting in the extended period of civil wars which blighted Yemen in the 1960s, fascinated me as a child.

He first fought in the highlands of Yemen. Then Egyptian President, Gamal Abdel Nasser, supported the revolutionary republicans with as many as 70,000 Egyptian troops and weapons in the civil war that raged in North Yemen from 1962 to 1970.

Egyptian troops were used against partisans of the kingdom who managed to dethrone the newly crowned Imam Muhammad al-Badr and declared Yemen a republic.

I couldn't get my father's stories out of my head so when I quit my job with Reuters in 2016, I finally made a trip to Yemen — to understand the country which had fascinated me since I was a child.

On my first visit in 2016, I saw how history was repeating itself in Yemen. The 'Imamate' regime which had ruled the country for centuries based on its religious authority was overthrown in favour of a republic in 1962.

The Houthi rebels at the heart of the current conflict are from the same Hashemite families which ruled Yemen for more than 1,000 years up until 1962. But in an added layer of complexity the Imamate's right to rule is not recognised by all Zaydis and some instead favour a republic.

Nearly 60 years later I found the followers of Ansar Allah, better known as the Houthis, were trying to restore the old system, arguing that their lineage to the Prophet entitled them to rule Yemen.

After the Houthis wrestled control of the Yemeni capital, Sana'a, in September 2014, and large areas in northern Yemen, many Yemenis fear that the group will establish the return of the Imamate.

Since the war started in Yemen in 2015 the country has experienced a humanitarian disaster. More than 370,000 people have died, including 150,000 deaths as a direct result of military action. More than 700,000 people have been injured or become sick, including mass outbreaks of cholera and an infrastructure collapse which has closed almost 50 percent of the country's hospitals.

Yemen's people are starving. As of 2024, the United Nations was seeking $2.7 billion to stave off hunger and disease for an estimated 18 million people, including 2.4 million acutely malnourished children.

I have visited Yemen on numerous occasions since 2016, reporting on the war there between its internationally recognised government, backed by Saudi Arabia and the United Arab Emirates, and the Houthi militia, a religious and political movement alleged to be receiving military support from Iran.

In April 2022, a truce was reached after a Saudi-Iranian agreement, according to which the front lines calmed down significantly, but not completely. Limited clashes

occurred, the most prominent of which was the Houthi strike on oil export platforms in what resembled a veto against the export of oil by the government unless they shared its profits. The Houthi attacks on Saudi Arabia and the coalition have stopped completely, except for a Houthi strike on a Bahraini military battalion at the end of 2023.

But the impact of the war has continued to be felt by the people of Yemen.

From 2022, there have been developments towards peace.

According to Maysaa Shuja Al-Deen, senior researcher at the Sana'a Center for Strategic Studies, the Houthi militia attack on the Saudi Aramco Bulk Plant, an oil facility, in March 2022 was certainly one of the most important reasons for Saudi Arabia to start negotiating with Iran for a truce, and in practice the truce did not occur until after the agreement with Iran. It was also Saudi Arabia's feeling that the Yemen war had exhausted it economically and politically, and its desire to move forward with Vision 2030, which requires guaranteeing stability and security of its lands from possible Houthi attacks.

Making matters worse is the ongoing conflict in Gaza which began on 7 October 2023 and which at the time of writing continues to reverberate across the region of the Middle East and in Yemen in particular. As the United States and Britain launched airstrikes against the Houthis for disrupting global shipping to protest the bombardment of Gaza, millions of Yemenis who

have already lost everything in the last decade are now farther away from their elusive dream of peace and stability. The activation of the Houthis as an Iranian arm is becoming obvious for the first time. The Houthis have been weaponised and financed 'cheaply' and the West now understands the dangers of Iran's proxies, including Houthis, after ignoring this for a long time and treating them as a Saudi problem.

This book is a combination of the photos I took through different trips to Yemen. The photos show everyday reality in a nation experiencing one of the world's longest running wars. The conflict may not be visible in every frame but it infuses all the images.

Right: Pro-government forces on a break between clashes with Houthi fighters in Taiz

The militias-run capital and the northern parts under their control

The people of the city where all women's faces are covered by a black niqab are protected by a pair of exposed 'Breasts': the local name for the twin peaks of the Al-Nahdeen mountain which tower over the Yemeni capital of Sana'a.

Situated in a mountain valley at an altitude of 2,200 metres Sana'a, Yemen's capital, is surrounded by various mountains, but its most notable is Al-Nahdeen to the south of the city. Known locally as 'the Breasts,' the peaks directly overlook the presidential complex keeping the huge stores of ballistic missiles kept there safe from raids by the Saudi-led coalition that opposes the city's new rulers.

So, despite the coalition launching hundreds of raids over the mountain, the stores were protected, and the Houthis continued hurling ballistic missiles at Saudi Arabia. Sana'a is controlled by the Houthi rebels (or 'Ansar Allah' militias – as Zaydi tribesmen commonly called the Houthis – under the leadership of Abdul-Malik al-Houthi).

They took advantage of the chaos following the Arab Spring in Yemen to take hold of Sana'a, in late 2014, driving the internationally-recognised government out of the capital. The movement burst into life in 2004 and found itself in multiple conflicts with the government. Saudi Arabia panicked.

It believed that the Houthis would gain support from the Shi'ite government in Iran, creating an enemy on its doorstep. So Saudi Arabia formed a coalition in early 2015 to reinstall the recently deposed president, Abd al-Rabbuh Mansur Hadi. Although the coalition was formed by a number of Arab countries and is headed by Saudi Arabia the ultimate backer is the US.

The intervention was codenamed Operation Decisive Storm, and started with a bombing campaign against the Houthis, before morphing into a naval blockade and forces on the ground in Yemen. The Saudi Arabian bombing campaign against the Houthi-led territories across Yemen caused mass civilian casualties.

When I flew to Sana'a, the Saudi-led coalition allowed flights to land in the capital city via Saudi Arabia, but by late 2016 they only allowed passengers to fly into the airports of Aden and Hadramout, which were under their control. They closed down airspace in San'a in August 2016.

Inside Sana'a, militiamen, many just youngsters, roamed the city wearing a mix of military jackets and the traditional Yemeni Mi'waz (a thin patterned cotton or linen fabric wrapped around the legs like a skirt) often replacing pants. They criss-crossed the city in pick-up trucks, flaunting weapons that look too big for a child to carry.

According to Human Rights Watch, the Houthis had intensified their recruitment and training of children since 2014 – when they took control of the Yemeni capital – and use them increasingly as scouts, guards, and fighters, with some children being wounded and killed. UNICEF also stated that children with the Houthis and other armed groups comprise up to a third of all fighters in Yemen.

Gun culture is a feature of Yemeni life, especially in the north. Even civilian men walk into restaurants and coffee shops with their Kalashnikovs, leaving their firearms on the side while eating. Even before the latest civil war it was estimated there were three times as many guns in Yemen as people.

I stayed in a small hotel on the main street. Outside, street vendors sold tactical vests and chest rigs, next to displays of janbiyas, the distinctly shaped traditional Yemeni dagger. Many shops were also doing brisk business selling solar panels to cope with the electricity shortages and power cuts that are a regular feature of Yemeni life. Solar panels are everywhere, at the markets, at homes, at checkpoints outside of the cities, and in rural areas. The Houthis deprived Yemenis of a normal life in order to profit from their miseries. They created a 'war economy' where instead of restoring electricity, the Houthis sold residents 'commercial electricity.' The same with fuel, where the Houthis monopolised the imports to areas under their control and sold it with skyrocketing prices to Yemenis.

Located in a mountain valley, the Old City of Sana'a in Yemen is one of the oldest cities in the world. It dates back about 2,500 years. It is marked by densely packed rammed earth and burnt tower-houses.

There is a big market for the spices Yemen is famous for, the same area is also full of 'martyr' photos: fighters who have been killed in the war with the Saudi-led coalition. In contrast there were – in 2016 at least – still also plenty of photos of the deposed former-president Ali Saleh.

Ali Abdullah Saleh was Yemen's longest-serving president and was in office for 33 years; two or three generations of people were born and lived under his rule but didn't know who he really was. He kept hold of power through a series of changing alliances; with the tribes, the military, and also the Islamist Brotherhood Islah (a loose confederation of tribal and religious groups with links to the Muslim Brotherhood). He was head of the General People's Congress which had been in power in Yemen since 1993.

In theory it was an Arab nationalist party but though it lacked an ideology and membership it enabled people to live and be employed. Ali Abdullah Saleh's party had strong support in many parts of northern Yemen. The malleable political instincts that enabled Saleh's long rule eventually proved his undoing. He fell out with Ali Muhsin al-Ahmar, his vice-president in 2011, after the autocrat took steps to install his son as successor, prompting the Islah leader to put his group's weight behind the Arab Spring protests in 2012, ending Saleh's rule.

When Yemen again fell into civil war in 2014 the deposed autocrat formed an alliance with his previous bitter enemies, the Houthis, in order to regain power. Saleh instructed military units still loyal to him to allow the Houthis free rein, enabling the Shi'a group to quickly dominate the north with its pick-up-truck-mounted army.

The Houthis belong to the Hashemite families from Zaydi (a branch of Shi'ite Islam) who controlled northern Yemen for centuries, through a royal bloodline. They managed to dominate Yemen despite accounting for

The twin peaks of the Al-Nahdeen Mountains, Arabic for 'The Two Breasts,' tower over the Yemeni capital of Sana'a.

just 10 percent of the country's population, claiming their right to rule on the basis that the country's leader has to be from the Hashemite family (those who are grandchildren of the Prophet).

According to Shuja Al-Deen, the Houthis as a group are trying to revive the legacy of the Imamate despite their apparent adherence to the republican system. They rely on the legacy of the Imamate, specifically in the element of restricting the leadership (Imamate) to the Hashemites, but they are currently calling for a relatively new concept in the Zaydi school of thought called 'guardianship,' which gives the leadership a spiritual quality and religious holiness that the traditional Zaydi Imam does not possess.

The Imamate was a near millennia-long system of government over an area which changed regularly depending on shifting tribal alliances and personal allegiances, with many areas in Yemen, including some of the Zaydis themselves, refusing to recognise the Hashemite right to leadership on the basis of being spiritual descendants of the Prophet Muhammed.

Throughout the history of Yemen, the Hashemites would come to power, rule the capital and parts of Yemen, then an uprising would break out against them and drive them back to their birthplace of Sa'ada.

Yemen may have been in chaos when I arrived but the Houthis had taken control of the media, assigning a minder to every journalist coming to the country. They allowed journalists to take pictures of the war-damaged infrastructure but not of security men, checkpoints or anything political. A minder from the Information Ministry drove me around the city, taking me where I wanted to go. But there was one rule: we always needed to stop work in the early afternoon so he could buy qat, a narcotic leaf that's used all through Yemen from midday until evening. People chew it from after lunch until late, using it as a social lubricant much like a group of French or Italians might share a bottle of wine.

The qat plant is native to Yemen and known for its addictive properties, users usually develop a habit that requires they start chewing on the leaf soon after lunch. Almost 70 percent of Yemenis, including women, chew on qat. As soon as lunch is finished, men fill the qat markets, and exchanges over the price of the plant sometimes get so heated you hear shots fired in the air.

Alcohol may be illegal in Yemen but qat is sold widely and it is acceptable to chew the plant while working, even for soldiers or security personnel. Men still make sure to empty their mouths of qat before praying. Qat also works as an informal means of exchange.

I had gone to Kawkaban, to the west of the capital to see a historical site damaged by the Saudi-led raids. When my minder ran out of money for the begging women who were carrying their babies, he offered them some of his qat instead.

Working in Yemen could be frustrating. A three-day trip in a four-wheel drive through the hilly areas of the country around Sa'ada – the birthplace of the Houthis – yielded nothing except a few pictures of places that had been damaged by the coalition raids. On the way we passed Amran, another northern province controlled by the Houthis.

The impact of the six wars which started in 2004, when former-president Saleh started fighting the Houthis, was clear. Bullet-riddled houses were seen along the highway, but I only managed to stop to take photos of men and women queuing for humanitarian aid. As I tried to reach the frontline in Hajja province, close to the border with Saudi Arabia, the minder interfered as usual.

Instead, I was taken to a small pre-prepared store, far from the fighting, where bullets and cluster bomb shrapnel were lined on the ground as evidence of the air raids. Paying for three days of travel wasn't cheap but I was too exasperated to complain at this point. Given that most of the cash was paying for the driver and the

minders' food and hotel bills I decided to accept the offer of some of their qat.

It was the first time I had tried the plant but chewing the bitter leaf calmed me down before I headed back to Sana'a. Back in the capital, I attended tribal gatherings which were intended to collect money and show support for the Houthis.

I also went to a huge gathering for the anniversary of the death of the group's one-time founder, Hussein Badreddin al-Houthi (killed in 2004 after months of battles between Yemeni security forces and the Houthis). It was a big celebration, conducted in separate halls, one each for male and female supporters, who were carrying banners and flags with photos of the leader who gave the movement its name.

It was late afternoon and a group of women had gathered at a dark place near the old town. The women were all clad in black.

At first, I thought it was a conservative gathering, then near the end a girl surprised me with an invite to her place the next day to chew qat with her and a group of friends. They would sit there on the top floor of her old building. They called the small rooftop Tayyara (airplane). Sat there chewing qat they feel as if they are flying in the air, free from the chaos below.

Right: A view of the old city of Sana'a, notable for its distinctive architectural character expressed in multistorey buildings decorated with geometric patterns.

Left: Photographs of pro-Houthi fighters killed during the clashes are displayed on a building in the old city of Sana'a.

Above: A woman peers out of the window of her home in the old city of Sana'a.

A woman and her daughter stand before the ancient, ornate Yemen Gate or 'babe l-Yemen,' which leads into Sana'a and dates back to the seventeenth century.

A mother sits on a hospital bed with her malnourished child awaiting a medical check-up in a hospital in Sana'a.

Right: Tactical military vests and chest rigs are on sale at a local market in the old city of Sana'a.

Left: A young man sits surrounded by spices on sale in the spice market with a photograph of the late former-president Ali Abdullah Saleh on display.

Above: A boy rides his bike past the qat market in the old city of Sana'a.

Men from the Arhab tribe arrive at a pro-Houthi ceremony on the outskirts of Sana'a.

The magazine of a man's weapon is adorned with images of martyrs in the war against the Saudi-led coalition.

Left: Men from the Arhab tribe raise their ceremonial janbiya daggers in the air in a show of support for the Houthis.

Above: A man and his child stand in front of a billboard of the late Houthi leader Hussein Badreddin al-Houthi during a commemoration event on the outskirts of Sana'a. The Houthi movement took his name after his assassination by the government in 2004.

Top left: Militia and a security guard at a checkpoint with a billboard showing a late Houthi leader, and another billboard with the Houthi slogan: 'God is the Greatest, Death to America, Death to Israel, Cursed be the Jews, Victory to Islam.'

Left: Supporters chant pro-Houthi slogans during a commemorative gathering for the late Hussein Badreddin al-Houthi.

Children and youths carrying weapons perform a tribal dance to zawamel songs to boost fighter morale.

A child joins his father at a meeting in Hasaba where pro-Houthi tribes gather to show their allegiance.

A fundraiser against the Saudi-coalition is held on the streets of Hasaba District in Sana'a. Followers leave local Yemeni currency, US dollars and bullets.

Above: A man with a pistol arrives at the commemorative gathering for the late Hussein Badreddin al-Houthi.

Top, left: Men tune up their weapons at the weapons market in Sana'a.

Right: A young boy rests between the pumps of a gas station in Sa'ada.

A youth stands guard with his weapon at a distribution site for humanitarian assistance.

A child soldier grasps his gun while sitting in the back of a pick-up truck at a gas station along the road near Hajja province. Child soldiers are used in northern Yemen to man checkpoints and provide security.

A man sells qat, while also chewing it, along the highway between Sa'ada and Hajja.

A young boy stands in the midst of qat sellers on the highway between Sa'ada and Hajja.

Women queue to receive humanitarian assistance
at the distribution point in Amran.

A girl adjusts her scarf while standing in front of a school in Sa'ada that was hit by the Saudi-led coalition.

Young female students attend class in a school in Sa'ada partially destroyed by air raids. The students were asked to veil themselves in front of the camera.

Women carry large plastic containers to fill them with drinking water. Yemen is one of the world's most water-stressed countries and suffers from lack of water supplies.

Left: Women visit the graves of their sons who fought with the Houthis against pro-government forces.

Above: A militiaman stands guard in an area bombed during a Saudi-coalition air raid on Haradh in Hajjah.

A solar panel placed on top of a damaged car provides power to a nearby security checkpoint in Hajjah.

A woman and child walk past the rubble of a millennia-old citadel at the entrance to Kawokaban, north-west of Sana'a.

The remains of a destroyed factory in the public services district in Sa'ada, the birthplace of the Houthis.

Left: A man looks out of his demolished building following an air raid by the Saudi-led coalition on a residential area in Sana'a.

Above: Displaced families living in makeshift tents in Amran province near Sana'a hang their clothes.

Men and young boys queue to receive humanitarian aid in Amran. Nearly 90 percent of Yemen's population relies on humanitarian assistance.

A displaced baby lays in a hammock inside a makeshift tent.

An internally displaced girl cooks outside of her family tent in the Haradh area of Hajja province, close to the Saudi Arabia border, that has witnessed clashes.

A woman walks past rubble in a Sa'ada district destroyed by Saudi-led coalition air raids.

Taiz: The City of Snipers

My hotel in Sana'a was packed with people from Taiz, a city high up in the Yemeni highlands in the south-west of the country. Nestling in the hills, 1,400 metres (4,600ft) above sea level, it is the capital of the Taiz Governorate.

The residents of the Sana'a hotel said they were escaping the fighting in Taiz between the Houthis – 'who were besieging the city' – and the pro-government forces backed by Saudi Arabia. Taiz is also a centre for human right activists and the supporters who toppled President Saleh's regime during the Arab Spring.

Because Taiz was the main centre of opposition to the Houthis I couldn't get there directly from Sana'a, and the Houthis wouldn't allow non-Yemenis to access it from areas under their control.

So, to get to Taiz I had to return to Egypt and re-enter Yemen from the pro-government stronghold of Aden. I headed from Aden to Taiz via the 'Mount Taluk' trail, built to open a route to the besieged city which bypassed Houthi checkpoints.

Before taking the Mount Taluk trail, I passed by Turba, an area on the outskirts of Taiz, packed with activists and opponents of the Houthis. A contact took me to see his family and the stock of weapons they had built up since the conflict started: an AK-47, and three other weapons, including rocket-propelled grenades. It was late in the day and leaving Taiz was difficult because none of the drivers wanted to tackle the narrow two-way path in darkness. They all wanted to wait until morning, but after I offered to pay in US dollars, one driver said he was willing to take me in a private car. As we pulled away, I

saw his cheeks were almost exploding from the amount of qat stuffed into his mouth. It was a stomach-churning journey as he steered his old car at high speeds for four hours along the mountain's edge.

In Taiz city, I was advised that staying at a hotel would attract attention, so instead I slept at the flat of a human rights activist who introduced me to her female friends. Some were heading to the front line to offer food and medicine to the fighters, like Reham, and other male friends were going there to fight, like Osama.

Every day I was waking up hearing the rockets as they hit both the outskirts and the centre of the city. Many residents were packing all they could onto pick-up trucks and were heading out of the city. I visited the hospitals; some of the injured had been fighting on the front line but the rest were residents of Taiz, hit by the mostly Russian-made mortars and Katyusha rockets fired by the Houthis and the Republican Guards of former-president Ali Saleh as they shelled the city from the hills around.

Snipers were active and indiscriminate, killing not just fighters but also activists and civilians. Once known as the 'cultural capital of Yemen,' Taiz is now the 'city of snipers.' Residents were regularly fired on if they accidentally passed into a sniper's sights as they crossed the hilly city. Many journalists and activists have been killed in Taiz since the war started.

The fighting has also devastated Taiz's main streets, hospitals, and even its architectural heritage. Places like the Cairo Citadel which was damaged by airstrikes in 2015 and the Taiz Museum, now used by pro-government

forces after its precious manuscripts were destroyed by shelling in 2016. Broken infrastructure means that power cuts are a fact of life in Taiz. The city's main streets were a ghost town of bullet-riddled walls and outright ruins from fighting between the Houthis and the pro-Salih Republican Guards. The faces of activists who have disappeared were painted on the walls of one of the city's main streets.

For centuries Taiz has been a centre of traditional Yemini heritage and crafts, home to philosophers and poets. It was also the home of political activism before Yemen's first republic was established.

The Islah 'Muslim Brotherhood' party was founded in 1990 in Sana'a and has much support in Taiz, a city which has the country's largest Sunni population. The Salafists, who follow the Salafi movement that exemplify a pure form of Islam and reject religious 'innovation' also has many followers in Taiz. Islah and Salafist supporters formed the bulwark of opposition to the Houthis in Taiz.

According to Shuja Al-Deen, all of the Islah party leaders since it was founded in 1990 are from the northern Zaydi regions, not Taiz or other Sunni regions. Islah has a wide presence all around Yemen, but for many reasons, Islah focused on Taiz. It also has a big presence in Marib and controls most of its administrative facilities. They participated extensively in the battle to defend Marib against the Houthis, and before that they were also participating in the battle of Aden against the Houthis. But they control Taiz, and their presence is strong in Marib.

The Salafist factions are also spread everywhere. The Abu Abbas Salafist factions tried to control Taiz, the city, and were prevented by forces loyal to the Islah 'Muslim Brotherhood.' The most important armed Salafist faction is the Giants Forces, who took part in the battle in Hodeidah.

The points above are very important and the conflict should not be seen as strictly Sunni opposed to Shi'ite. Yemen is not like Iraq in this divide and the reader needs to know that it is a multi-layered conflict in Yemen. Not all the Zaydis agree with the Houthis, and many Zaydis can be members of the Muslim Brotherhood as they like their ideas, which does not happen in Shi'ite Iraq or Iran.

The city was still full of activists, leftists, socialists, even Nasserists espousing the pan-Arab nationalism of the former Egyptian president, all of whom protested during the Arab Spring uprising. I found a student battalion, made up of people who never imagined holding a pistol in their hands but had no choice but to defend their city. Many of the activists were anti-Islamists: Islah and Salafists. There were also some who had fought in Afghanistan against the Soviets. I even heard that a few Al-Qaeda members took part in the fighting. Diverse groups, united against a common foe.

Naseem, the activist, introduced me to her uncle, a former officer who learned in Iraq how to dismantle mines during the Iraq-Iran war. He helped me visit the front lines and speak to the fighters there. He had lost one son in the war a year earlier and now his youngest son was involved in the fighting. I saw many young men who had lost limbs to mines and the officer was using his

A pro-government fighter stands guard near barricades in a deserted residential area amidst renewed clashes between the Houthis and pro-government forces.

landmine detector to teach the fighters how to find these weapons. The Houthis plant mines extensively before retreating and the young untrained fighters often rush in without checking, said Captain Taher.

In Taiz the magic of nature and beauty of the green hilly areas contrasts vividly with the effects of combat and the destruction from all the fighting on its land.

I was taking an evening walk with some female activists, chatting about when the war would end. Reham, in common with some young women in Taiz, doesn't cover her face, unlike most Yemeni women. She complained of the Islamists' influence on this open-minded city of culture as many women in Taiz and Aden don't cover their faces.

One evening in Taiz, I was drinking mango juice with some activists, discussing an upcoming prisoner swap. Our gathering at the cafeteria caught the attention of extremist Islah lawmaker Abdullah al Odeiny, who tweeted about this 'outrageous' example of gender-mixing. He was so annoyed by the moral decay of people drinking juice together that he dedicated his next Friday prayer speech to the subject.

The prisoner swap event took place just after this but the activists didn't tell me about it because they were scared by Odeiny's speech. I left Taiz two days later.

I have covered conflicts all over the Middle East but nowhere has horrified me like Taiz. I saw young victims of landmines and artillery shells who were still soldiers, even with limbs missing, because it's shameful in their culture for men not to fight. Those young men were dying every day without any attention from the international community, access to prosthetic limbs or other medical help. Many Yemenis come to Egypt for treatment and later I met one of them in a Cairo hospital: he was an engineer from Taiz who had lost his hands, legs and eyesight trying to defuse a landmine planted in front of a residential building.

A few months later, two of the activists I met in Taiz were killed by snipers, almost simultaneously near the front line: Reham was shot as she went to hand out aid boxes. Osama died during one of innumerable clashes between the opposing sides.

I went back to Taiz in May 2018, six months after former-president Salih was killed by the Houthis, and two years after I had initially visited it. Islah and the Salafists were fighting in the streets, but instead of attacking the Houthis now they were fighting each other. When I first went to Taiz, both Islah and Salafists forces were fighting the Houthis, but two years later, they were confronting each other in the city's streets. This shows the proxy nature of war in Yemen; Islah is backed by Saudi Arabia and the Salafist leaders are financed by the UAE. This drove a wedge among different factions in Taiz.

Saudia Arabia supported the Islah party, which forms the biggest part of the legitimate government and the main component of its forces, the UAE, who detested the Muslim Brotherhood backed Islah's opponents, the reactionary Sunni Salafists. While Saudi Arabia has supported the Islah party since the 1960s, other allegiances were more malleable.

I met Captain Taher again, he was still working hard to clear the country of landmines and explosives. Some of the front lines were quieter but the fighting continued. Months later I heard news that Captain Taher had died from a direct hit by a Houthi missile, when he was dismantling a mine around the outskirts of Marib.

Even today, Taiz is considered under siege; Houthi forces are present on the eastern sides, towards Al-Hawban and Ibb. The 'Mount Taluk' path is still used but other routes are out in the open and surrounded by the Houthis.

Right: Yemeni men riding a jeep cross the trail at Taluq to bypass Houthi checkpoints.

Anti-Houthi fighters in Taiz in search of mines in an area recently freed from Houthi control.

A pro-government fighter fires his machine gun from the rooftop of a building at Houthi positions in Taiz.

A pro-government fighter changes his position during a shootout with Houthi fighters in Taiz.

A government T-55 tank, manned by anti-Houthi fighters, fires at Houthi positions in Taiz.

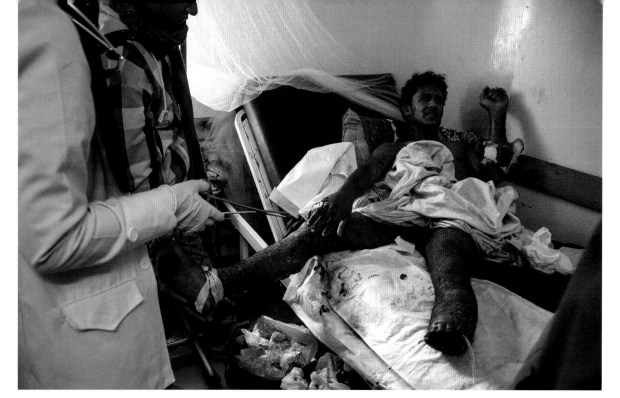

A young fighter badly injured by a Houthi mine is treated in hospital in Taiz.

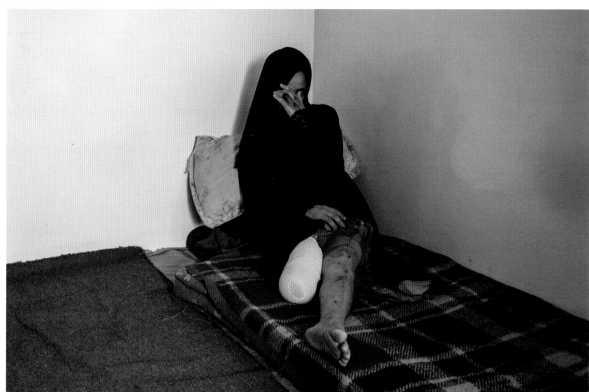

A 24-year-old woman who stepped on a Houthi mine next to her home receives treatment in hospital in Taiz.

A father and his infant daughter with shrapnel injuries covering their bodies sit in hospital awaiting treatment.

A prosthetics lab in Taiz hospital designs artificial limbs to support those injured in the war.

An old woman with her grandchild, injured in the war, sit at home in Taiz.

A boy walks past an unexploded mortar bomb that has been demarcated with rocks by residents in Taiz.

Injured fighters in Taiz rest during combat.

Above: A father weeps over the body of his dead son surrounded by his comrades in Taiz.

Top left: A government officer defuses a landmine inside the house of a Yemeni man in Taiz.

Left: A young man fires shots in the air ahead of his late friend's funeral in Taiz.

Above: Pro-government fighters take a stroll in a deserted neighbourhood destroyed by the war in Taiz.

Top left: A family and all their belongings piled on top of a jeep leave Taiz during the war.

Left: A young widow of a recently deceased fighter stands at the entrance of her home with her children in Taiz.

Inside a qat market men gather to sell the narcotic.

Mocha: The Fall from Grace

The city of Mocha on the Red Sea coast of Yemen, part of the Taiz governorate, was for centuries one of the world's greatest ports, a major trade centre under the Ottomans and the focal point of Yemen's 200-year global coffee trade monopoly. Mocha is also very close to the Bab-el-Mandeb, or the Gate of Grief, a strait between Yemen and Africa that connects the Red Sea to the Gulf of Aden. When the British conquered its competitor Aden in 1839, they made it their primary harbour.

Decades of neglect and war have left Mocha's port empty, with ships sailing for Hodeidah and Aden instead, leaving Mocha to become merely a smuggling centre for goods and refugees. The smuggling activity has shrunk since the area became a military zone for the coalition, but for years boats came from the Horn of Africa via Mocha, full of African migrants.

Houthi militias took over Mocha during their military offensive in March 2015, but pro-government troops retook the town in early 2017. Now Mocha is a base for troops fighting the Houthis on Yemen's Red Sea coast. Mocha was where the central command for the UAE's operations was located before they left in 2019, and it is still the main base for UAE-backed Tariq Saleh militias that are fighting the Houthis.

I went to Mocha in May 2018 because it was where journalists gathered to travel to Hodeidah where the fighting between Houthis and pro-government forces to take over the port city was intensifying. When I went to the press centre in Mocha, the building was packed with Salafist fighters and it was difficult as a woman to base myself or stay there as male journalists were able to. Because there were only two small hotels at that time, and security issues, the media centre tried to help me find accommodation with a family.

I stayed for a few days with a wife of one of the fighters from Aden near an old area with washed away houses; filled with displaced people running from the fighting in other areas of Yemen.

Many of them were waiting for the fighting to be over so they can return to their villages in nearby cities. Around 90 percent of the inhabitants in Mocha are not from the city; they are mostly members of the different fighting groups as well as displaced people. Displacement camps were spread in many areas of the city, most of the displaced people came from Hodeidah because of the clashes but there were many from other areas who fled the fighting in Taiz and other cities earlier. They took over rundown old buildings in the city to live in.

The living conditions in Yemen's slummy camps for displaced people are very bad. Many of their inhabitants are forced to collect garbage for recycling to earn money while countless children are visibly malnourished. Women walk long distances in the morning for firewood because they have no stoves or propane gas to cook with, while many of them have lost their husbands on the battlefield or have had them detained as prisoners of war.

Fishing and boat building remain major industries in Mocha, even though it was affected by the fighting and the military bases of the coalition which limits the fishermen's mobility. Electricity supplies are erratic due to a neglected and malfunctioning power plant.

Lack of organised trips for journalists to the front line led me to move from Mocha and head to Al-Khokha town in Hodeidah, which had been liberated from the Houthis. I left with a local Hodeidah resistance fighter in his pick-up truck and he offered to put me up in Al-Khokha where his family lives. Like many fighters' families they had rented an apartment in Al-Khokha, which was now a safe town, while their relatives headed for the frontline.

A man in a workshop paints a traditional boat in Mocha.

Mocha's mayor (right) meets with residents during a qat chewing session in his house.

Above: Displaced children living in a makeshift tent play next to a solar panel used to generate power.

Right: Displaced children collect garbage and sift through public waste for recyclable items in Mocha.

Above: A displaced woman bakes bread in a clay oven outside of her tent.

Top left: Women in a makeshift camp collect firewood for cooking.

Left: Yemeni girls attend a workshop for children affected by the war, organised by NGOs in Mocha.

Hodeidah and the Battle for the West Coast

Hodeidah is the second largest port in Yemen after Aden, but its proximity to Yemen's population centres meant 70 percent of Yemen's imports went through the port. Yemen imports 90 percent of its goods, especially foods and medicine. Hodeidah is also the largest agricultural and industrial region in Yemen.

As the Houthi rebels controlled the port, the UN and the coalition started monitoring ships using the facility. The logistical impact of this saw trade shift to other places with goods starting to come through Aden or Mukalla port (in Hadramout), or via land crossings through neighbouring Saudi Arabia and Oman.

The Saudis have has subjected Yemen to a sea, land and air blockade imposed since it started its military intervention in Yemen in 2015. The United States joined the blockade in October 2016 and increased its support to Saudi Arabia with fuel, equipment, and weapons. The blockade ratcheted up further in 2017, after the Houthis launched a missile from Yemen towards Riyadh.

The result was a humanitarian catastrophe for the Yemenis and prompted the United Nations to declare that Yemen was facing the world's worst famine. The World Health Organization said that over half a million Yemenis had become infected with cholera. During the blockade, Yemen did not receive any foreign aid or assistance through its main port of Hodeidah. Fuel supplies, however, still made it on to the dockside. The blockade lasted from 2015 till late 2022.

I arrived at Al-Khokha as forces backed by the UAE tried to take the strategic port of Hodeidah from the Houthis in the summer of 2018. The local resistance, known as the 'Tihama Brigades' (named after the nearby countryside) were already fighting the Houthis to free Hodeidah. The Tihama fighters wear the traditional Yemeni sarongs and sandals when they fight. They threw their lot in with the UAE-backed Southern Forces in 2018 in a bid to take the port.

The UAE also backed a brigade led by Tariq Abdallah Saleh, the nephew of former-president Ali Abdullah Saleh (Yemen's long-time autocrat removed by a popular uprising in 2012) to fight alongside the Southern Forces against the Houthis. But members of the local Tihama Brigade refused to ally with combatants who were formerly part of the national army that had once opposed them.

Marwan, a 19-year-old fighter who was based in the port town of Khokha, south of Hodeidah, told me that the coalition had provided four months of training for all the groups, in the islands of Zuqar and Hanish. They were also provided with guns but they seemed to feel that all parties needed more weaponry. Marwan said that before the other forces came to Hodeidah: 'There was always a resistance from inside the province secretly without support or money. We just didn't accept the Houthis, we already felt marginalised by the Zaydis who were in charge of all major ranks during the former regime,' he said, referring to the Shi'ite sect to which both the Houthis and former-president Mr Saleh belonged.

As a Tihama Brigade member, he has reservations about the resistance fighting alongside Mr Saleh's forces, who until recently were allied with the Houthis.

The battle to take Hodeidah was at its peak when I arrived. The UAE has funded the fighters of all groups and they were all determined to retake the port. When I joined Tarek Saleh's forces, I also saw piles of qat, obviously necessary for the Yemeni fighter, I was told it was also paid for by the UAE.

The family members I stayed with were very happy that the fighters were closing in on the airport, which is very near to their house in Hodeidah. They said they were hoping to return home soon. The combat was fierce with the fighters talking about 'thermal missiles' used by the Houthi forces. The coast was littered with landmines and there are few, if any records, of where they had been planted. A Tihama commander I interviewed was killed by a landmine a few days after we spoke.

It wasn't easy to reach the front line but many times I got help from the local fighters. Tareq's forces appeared to be the best trained as they used to be part of the regular army during the former regime and they accepted journalists, unlike the Salafists members who were fighting fiercely but were cautious of the media. I was still able to take photos with all groups when there were no hard-line Salafi members present.

The anti-Houthi forces were advancing during the time I stayed there. As I was leaving, fighters reached Al-Durayhimi area, which is 15 kilometres away from the main city of Hodeidah (capital of Hodeidah province). Then they advanced into the city, encircled it from the south and east, cut off the Hodeidah-Sana'a main road, and took control of almost half of the port city. Only three kilometres separated them from controlling Hodeidah port when the signing of the Stockholm Agreement between the legitimate government and the Houthis stopped the battle. This left the forces remaining in the positions that they controlled, and the war stopped except for light skirmishes, as an international truce entered into force and a UN team supervised the agreement's implementation.

The situation was stable until November 2021, when the legitimate joint forces withdrew from the city of Hodeidah and from the coastal line that it controlled, and stationed themselves in the city of Khokha and Hais, which is about 150 kilometres from the city of Hodeidah.

The agreement stipulated that the two parties withdraw 20 kilometres and the Houthis hand over the ports of Hodeidah to the local authority that existed before the group invaded the city in 2014, but they did not implement any of the terms of the agreement. Rather, they restored their control over the areas from which the legitimate forces withdrew.

A commander in the government forces told me they're bigger than the forces from the Houthis 'Still, we represent many armies,' he said.

I kept in touch with the family and the fighters at Al-Khokha after I left. They are still staying in the rented apartments hoping to return to their homes.

On 2 April 2022, the warring parties agreed to a two-month truce initiated by the United Nations, which included an agreement to stop all offensive military operations, allow fuel ships to enter Hodeidah ports and to resume commercial flights from Sana'a airport. Although the truce has resumed, the situation with the militias and the displaced people remains.

Pro-government fighters ride motorbikes in the countryside of Taiz close to the border with Hodeidah.

Pro-government forces prepare ahead of clashes with Houthi fighters in Taiz.

Pro-government fighters in Hodeidah near the west coast engage in combat, firing from their military base at Houthi positions, and attend to their injured.

Left: A pro-government fighter strolls along the shore of the Yemeni west coast past the corpses of fighters killed in clashes with the Houthis.

Above: A member of the Tihama Brigade is seen near a frontline position in Hodeidah.

A pro-government mine clearer locates and detonates mines found in areas recaptured from Houthi fighters.

Left: The body of a dead fighter lays strewn on the road after combat in Al Waze'yia in Taiz near Hodeidah.

Above: A Houthi is captured and made a prisoner of war by pro-government forces in Hodeidah.

Pro-government forces take shelter underneath a pier hit
by a Saudi-coalition airstrike at Hodeidah's harbour.

Pro-government fighters chew qat under the shade of an MRAP during a lull in fighting in Hodeidah.

People caught in the crossfire of the conflict in Hodeidah leave their homes with their belongings in search for safety, with some receiving emergency assistance from pro-government forces.

Aden: The Dream of the South

Aden is the second largest city in Yemen, and since 2015, it's been the capital of the internationally-recognised government. The port of Aden was once a cosmopolitan city, its strategic position between the Arabian Sea and the Suez Canal meant it was once one of the world's busiest ports. It was also the centre of trade in Yemen especially under British rule, but administrative issues and a series of conflicts have seen it lose relevance to Dubai.

It's a centre for fishermen and a stopping point for ships travelling to India via the Horn of Africa. The city still has huge fish markets where you can buy many types of fish, large and small. In 1839 Britain's East India Company took control of Aden and ruled it out of what was then known as Bombay. Aden was a melting pot of people from the north of Yemen, the Gulf and numerous other nationalities such as Somalis and Indians. The 130 years of British rule have left their mark on Aden which is full of schools as well as churches, synagogues, and Hindu temples.

The city became the centre for education in Yemen and opposition to the Imamate (Zaydi rulers). It also attracted many leftists during the socialist times. Aden was the first city in the country to see a thriving newspaper industry. It was also a base for activists and leaders of movements and political parties during the former regime. Aden's oldest district Crater, is a neighbourhood known for its mix of Indian architecture and traditional Yemeni houses. Somalis, Indians, and Farsis – people from modern day Iran – all lived in Aden. The city was a melting pot of people, religions and ideas. The Jewish population in Yemen numbered up to 100,000 until the 1940s. However, the recent conflict has changed this; Salafi extremists and Al-Qaeda members destroyed a synagogue and a Farsi temple in the old town.

The Indian influence can be felt in the popular Adani tea with milk, which is more common in Aden's cafes than the coffee which Yemen is famous for. Spicy food is characteristic of all Yemen but especially in Aden where you can experience both African and Asian dishes.

Now Aden is the capital of the internationally-recognised government and a base for political movements' leaders and military commanders, since the Houthis took control of Sana'a in September 2014. Since the civil war started it has attracted a large number of journalists and activists. And for me it was the base where I could travel to other cities in Yemen, especially after the Saudi-led coalition forced passengers to fly only into the Aden and Hadramout airports which were under their control. Aden is a much easier city to navigate than Sana'a and unlike the country's traditional capital, I didn't have a minder at my side at all times.

Aden was also the capital of the only communist-ruled Arab State: The People's Democratic Republic of Yemen, which existed between 1967 and 1990. Aden's importance increased when the country was sliced into two parts: North and South Yemen. The South's political leanings saw it allied with the Soviet Union, drawing it into the Cold War which defined the post-Second World War global order. At that time, it was a base for socialists and it welcomed left-wing activists from Syria, Iraq, and Egypt, especially before Yemen was unified in 1990.

From the first time I visited Aden, I noticed how many Yemenis in Aden are nostalgic for the socialist period, when Yemen was separated from the north. Many told me how women were much freer then, even today many women in Aden don't cover their faces unlike the rest of the country where it is standard. The manager at a sea-side hotel in Khormaksar and his employees talked about how things were better in the past: 'when someone could be detained if he's cheating on prices,' and where women were free to mix with men, without covering their faces. The manager didn't like the restrictions put on women after the unification of the two Yemens in 1990. 'It brought in old conservative traditions from the north,' he told me.

Flags of what used to be the People's Democratic Republic of Yemen, or South Yemen, are found everywhere; throughout the markets and at different checkpoints. It's the same flag used when Yemen gained independence from Britain. It consists of the three equal horizontal red, white, and black bands of the Arab Liberation flag, with a sky-blue triangle and a red star. It's now being used by the Transitional Council which wants to be free again from the north. Others, however, think it's better to reduce conflict and to stay united.

Saleh united North and South Yemen in 1990. This saw a war erupt in southern Yemen in 1994, after the new

Left: Fishermen plying their trade with nets in the Gulf of Aden.

president eliminated the socialist party, Salih's forces took complete control in tandem with his then allies, the Islah party.

As Saleh was busy in the early 2000s fighting the Houthis, a separatist movement reemerged in the south, finally taking their chance during the civil war when the Houthis took control of the north.

After the liberation of Aden from Houthi forces in 2015 following a three-month occupation, the internationally-recognised government took Aden as its capital. President Abdrabbuh Mansour, who came after Salih and was in office from 2012 to 2022, asked Aidarus al-Zoubaidi, an ex-South Yemen military commander who fled the country in 1994 to return and form a force to liberate the south and to secure Aden from Al-Qaeda elements.

Al-Zoubaidi's forces, mainly formed from forces of the pro-southern movement from the neighbouring Dali governorate, which was later officially declared as the Southern Transitional Council (STC) in 2017. But from 2015, the separatists started to clash with government forces in Aden.

Hadi government troops and STC forces took part in vicious fighting for control of Aden's airport, causing it to be closed down on multiple occasions. On my first visit to Aden in 2016 the airport was closed forcing us to change flights to Hadramout. In 2019 the STC forces finally evicted the Hadi troops from Aden and since then the airport has been open without interruption.

Control of Aden is divided between the legitimate government, mostly from the Islah Party and the STC. The STC was essentially a creation of the UAE. The Emiratis also formed the Security Belt Forces, composed of paramilitaries and the elite and military wing of STC, numbering 60,000 in total, with the aim of controlling those areas in Aden and confronting the influence of the Muslim Brotherhood. The UAE also formed the Southern Forces: mostly made up of Salafists. The UAE has supported the reactionary Salafists against Islah (Muslim Brotherhood) with money and military training and fought Hadi forces in Aden.

Two military confrontations took place between the STC and President Hadi's forces in Aden. In 2018, southern separatists backed by the UAE turned against the Riyadh-backed Presidential Guard, seizing Hadi's abandoned palace in Aden after a week of bloody clashes. The attempt to exclude Hadi failed as Saudi Arabia intervened.

When in August 2019 the STC managed to drive Hadi forces out of Aden, Hadi asked Saudi Arabia to get the UAE out of Yemen. Abu Dhabi complied, but the UAE continued to arm the Southern Forces and the STC. This resulted in the STC controlling Aden while the government forces affiliated with Hadi and the Islah party have power over neighbouring Shabwa and part of Abyan.

After several visits to Aden, I noticed increasing divides among the anti-Houthi forces. In late 2019 I met with Fadhel al-Gade, assistant secretary-general of the

STC's presidential council in Aden. He said that the STC wants the entire southern region including the areas of Aden, Shabwah, Hadhramaut, Lahij, Socotra, Abyan, Al-Dhali and Al-Mahrah governorates to return to a unitary southern state. 'We believed in unity and Arab nationalism for a while but then our southern people suffered from terrible living conditions after 1990 so that we are willing to sacrifice now in order to go back to being a single state,' he said.

While I was in Aden, I managed to get permission to join a military force for the day, who were responsible for Lahj province, another area that fell under the control of the STC located on north and west of Aden, between Taiz and Aden. It was a contact line with the Houthis. This area protects Aden and it's on the Red Sea close to the Bab-el-Mandeb strait.

Al-Dhali governorate neighbouring Aden was still an active war front line between Southern Forces and the Houthi militia, who were still shelling the governorate. During my visit to Aden in late 2019, I asked STC spokespeople if I could travel with them to Al-Dhali to visit the site of a military gathering at a stadium the Houthis had shelled the day before. There was a sudden visit of a Saudi-led coalition officer, who was probably surprised to find a photographer there, and soon after the STC spokespeople asked me to leave Aden as I didn't have a proper official visa for the media.

Right: A fisherman in Aden holds up a large fish like an assault rifle as a child looks on.

The Cisterns of Tawila, dating back many hundreds of years, that collected and stored the rain in the past to prevent flooding.

The neighbourhood of Crater in Aden early on a Friday morning.

Left: Kids play volleyball in a neighbourhood in Aden badly hit by the Saudi-led coalition.

Above: A pro-separatist man (centre) in Aden dons the pre-unity flag of the Republic of the South of Yemen.

Above, left: Members of the Southern Transitional Council Forces stand guard in Daleh near Aden.

Right: Young boys in Aden walk past a billboard showing Aidarus al-Zoubaidi, President of the Southern Transitional Council and de facto leader of the Southern Movement in Yemen.

Male and female members of the Southern Transitional Council security forces stand guard at 'Abyan gate,' the main checkpoint in the eastern part of the city of Aden. Violent confrontations between Houthis and later between government forces and the forces of the Transitional Council took place here.

Pro-government forces occupy and monitor frontline positions in Lahj City, a buffer zone protecting Aden from Houthi attacks.

Left, above: A qat market in Aden on New Year's Eve 2020 during which the price of the narcotic tripled.

African migrants smuggled from their countries via the Red Sea arrive in Bab-el-Mandab and walk 100 kilometres to reach Aden. Thousands of migrants from Africa cross through Yemen en route to the Gulf states to find work. Some are recruited into combat by Houthi fighters before reaching their final destinations.

A bakery on the outskirts of Aden servicing
local restaurants and residents.

Marib: Oil and War

The historic city of Marib was once the capital of the ancient Kingdom of Sheba. Old and new now sit side by side: the city's modern dam is close to the ruins of the eighth century BCE Great Dam of Marib. It's located in the closest pro-government province to the Houthi-controlled areas in the north, and it is the only city in that part of Yemen that remains under government control.

Marib has a key oil refinery that produces 90 percent of the country's liquefied petroleum gas. Just as in the civil war of the 1960s, the tribes in Marib and northern Yemen have played a decisive role in the current conflict, siding with the government as soon as fighting broke out.

Some of the Marib tribes reject the Zaydi claim to rule Yemen and fighting has been a fact of life in the areas in between the city and the Yemeni capital Sana'a. A banner on the city's main road features a portrait of the Marib man who killed the then-leader of Yemen, known as the 'Imam,' during the civil war of the 1960s.

Marib has changed dramatically in recent years. During the former regime it was an almost forgotten outpost, ruled by tribes and lacking basic services but funding from the Saudi-led coalition fighting the Houthis has changed this. Now services are available, large camps have been built for people displaced by the fighting, and the city itself has become a centre of military operations.

There has been an influx of over two million Yemenis to Marib and its surrounding towns since the conflict started in 2015, as people flee to escape the fighting or persecution. A senior employee of the Yemeni government's Executive Unit for Managing Displacement

Camps, who had himself lost a limb to a landmine, estimated that 65 percent of the country's five million internally displaced people now live in Marib province, either in tented camps or rental accommodation.

The biggest camp in Marib is Al-Jufaina, which is home to more than 75,000 internally displaced people. Residents say basic services in Marib are better than in other cities. The Al Sawida camp sits roughly 15 kilometres from Marib; established in early 2020 it's now home to thousands of families from all over Yemen. Despite frequent sandstorms and the ever-present threat of renewed Houthi offensives, residents of these camps say they are in Marib to stay.

The camps contain a mixture of people; some who left their villages to flee the fighting, former government soldiers escaping persecution, and others who simply say they have no choice but to remain in the last government stronghold in the war-torn country's north.

I found a driver to take me to the ruins of the ancient Barran Temple, also called the Throne of Bilqis, the very place where the Queen of Sheba used to sit. Rashad, 25, hails from Dhamar province, an area to the southwest of Marib and one which is now under Houthi control. He left his home in Dhamar eight years ago so he could finish his studies and to avoid being forcibly recruited by the Houthis. He now works as a microbus driver to pay his rent and the fees for studying business administration at Marib University. Rashad told me that before the war he would never have thought of living in Marib, a city well known for its outlaws under the previous Salah regime,

when it was a no-man's land without any services. Today Marib is a relative sanctuary, giving its residents a degree of security to work and invest.

Because of its closeness to the Houthi-controlled areas, the city is full of intelligence officers, who constantly stopped me when I was taking photos, even when I was accompanied by Yemeni minders. Marib, like Sana'a and other cities in the north of the country, is known for the jambiya; the Yemeni dagger is a ubiquitous sight in the city, while both civilians and soldiers also carry guns around.

Every town in Yemen has a weapons market. I was trying to find Marib's as I was taking photos in the janbiya market. A plain clothed security operative was spooked hearing me talking about weapons as I photographed a man on the street sewing machine gun covers. I was then taken by security car to a police station where my photos were checked but when they saw it was just ordinary pictures of a market, they released me. I told him I didn't think weapons would be an issue since all men in the country were carrying weapons.

Going to the front line was inevitable, as the fighting was intensifying between government forces and the Houthis on the outskirts of Marib. The government officials accompanying me first brought me to a safe area and then almost to the front line itself, where they offered me some staged photos of soldiers pretending to fire their weapons. Instead, I asked to meet some of the fighters at the second line to the front line where they could be still on alert or resting on the battlefield.

The Marib frontline has fighters from all around Yemen. Many soldiers were part of the army during the Salih regime who then fled the northern part of the country when it fell under Houthi control and are now staying in the displaced persons' camps. Some were prisoners of war, released as part of the prisoner swaps that are a feature of the conflict. There was also a regiment of hardened soldiers hailing from the Al Bayda region to the south of Yemen. When the Houthis took over their home province, they moved to Marib to continue the fight.

I met a military leader with a glass eye which replaced the one he lost to a bullet many years earlier. He said the bullet was still lodged in his skull. The fighters don't receive good medical treatment; as long as they are ready to fight again they head back to the front line; in any case most can't afford the cost involved in treating their wounds properly. As I left the front line I took a few photos of soldiers outside the conflict areas, including the one-eyed military leader.

My military media minders pulled over on the journey back to the city to buy qat. As I started to take photos a security man stopped me.

Before I left Marib I asked to see a wedding; wedding studios in the city had many photos of bridegrooms carrying their guns and their traditional janbiya daggers, another sign of the weapon's importance in the north of Yemen. I found a wedding the next day. In Yemen men and women celebrate weddings separately and as expected I could only attend the male gathering. A relative of the bridegroom had one arm in a fresh plaster cast having recently been shot fighting on the front line.

He told me how the Saudi-led coalition provided the fighters with weapons but also controlled their tactics, stopping their advances when they broke through the Houthi lines. Once, the government forces had managed to reach the outskirts of Sana'a itself before coalition airplanes forced them to halt. I had heard similar stories in Hodeidah province. The injured soldier told me that the war would last a long time.

Yemeni women take photographs at a historic site in Marib known as the Throne of the Queen of Sheba or the Barran Temple.

A Dust storm sweeps across
the highway in Marib.

Displaced women struggle through a dust storm to reach water points in a makeshift camp in Marib.

Women stand over a shared oven baking bread.

A young child looks on while women line up to receive humanitarian assistance in Marib.

Children in a displaced persons' camp
in Marib play and collect water.

At a school in Marib where the flag of united Yemen features with the words: 'God, Revolution, Nation, Unity.'

A pro-government military commander at a military base close to a frontline position.

Right: A soldier sits in a battered ambulance taking a rest during a lull in fighting in Marib.

Pro-government forces engage in combat at frontline positions contested by the Houthis inside Marib and near the border with Sana'a.

A pro-government fighter at
the frontlines in Marib takes
aim at Houthi positions.

In Marib, a man selling the traditional janbiya daggers poses inside his shop.

A child adjusts his janbiya dagger belt in Marib.

Left: A child holds up a rifle in a room where a
Yemeni groom readies himself for his wedding.

Above: A Yemeni groom draws his sword and adjusts
his attire ahead of wedding celebrations.

A Yemeni groom is surrounded by male attendees celebrating at his wedding.

Al Bayda: An Eternal Battlefront

History and geography have made Yemen's Al Bayda province a restless battlefield. It has a strategic location in the centre of the country, bordering seven major governorates: oil-rich Marib, Abyan, Damar, Ibb, Al-Dhalea, Shabwa and Sana'a, a rural area adjacent to the capital city itself. The Sunni-dominated area of Al Bayda has a long history of conflict with the Zaydis' Imamate rule. The region is characterised by a martial culture and the presence of violent tribes which has left a psychological impact on both the Sunnis and Zaydis.

Al Bayda is also close to the Shabwa and Abyan governorates which have been the main centres for Al-Qaeda and other extremist religious groups since they first appeared in Yemen in 1990. There's also an overlap of the social structure between the three governorates which were historically affiliated to South Yemen. This complex social and geographical overlap has made Al Bayda a shelter for Al-Qaeda which has been very active in the region and is still present there now.

The Houthis controlled only parts of Al Bayda at the start of the latest civil war. The pro-government forces initially managed to control the main road that connects the centre of the province with its most important city, Radaa. The anti-Houthi forces advanced from the direction of both Marib and Shabwa to the very centre of Al Bayda. The Saudi-backed coalition then cynically cut off their supplies: an act of realpolitik borne out of the large numbers of Al-Qaeda in their ranks who Riyadh hoped would fall to Houthi bullets and shells.

In most parts of Yemen Wednesday is an ordinary day but Al Bayda's people are superstitious about this 24-hour period because of the Ribou Incident. The word is Yemeni slang for Wednesday and it was on that day of the week in 1863 that the Zaydis invaded, their leader, the Imam, exploited sectarian rivalries to wrest control of the region from its then Ottoman rulers. The Zaydis killed a thousand Al Bayda soldiers and took another thousand prisoners, making their captives carry the heads of their dead comrades back to the Imam's capital to the north of Sana'a; an atrocity which the region's people still remember to this day.

The presence of Al-Qaeda elements in Al Bayda and a brief appearance of ISIS members in the governate has worsened the situation in Al Bayda in recent years, making this region one of the most dangerous fronts in the war. The Houthis had gained the upper hand when I visited Al Bayda in 2018 with the governate's defenders telling me that the Shi'ite group controlled almost 70 percent of the region.

There were still a few villages in Al Bayda that fought on against the Houthis and it was possible to reach them from Aden while avoiding the anti-government checkpoints. I travelled from the port city in a microbus with other passengers after an Aden-based activist from Al Bayda arranged for some of its soldiers to meet me at a certain point on the journey.

Despite the appearance of Al-Qaeda and other Islamic extremists in the governate, the bulk of its defenders

were not linked to any organisation, intelligence service or ideology. The soldiers there told me they didn't receive any external funding. But still they fought on. I met Ahmed Omar in Dhi Naim, a village in the south of Al Bayda where the fighters were still battling the Houthis. Omar, who was 33 at that time, led the fighting in the village. He used to work in Saudi Arabia, owning a house-painting company employing a number of his relatives. But when he heard the Houthis were attacking areas close to his family home, he returned to Yemen, bringing his colleagues with him, turning them from house painters to soldiers who fought the rebels on the slopes outside their village.

Yemeni expats living in Saudi Arabia financed the fight against the Houthis in Dhi Naim village, which was just three kilometres from a strategic highway which connects Al Bayda with Sana'a. The fighters were trying to wrestle control of this road from the Houthis in order to prevent the anti-government group from resupplying its troops in Al Bayda. Omar said he had contacted the Saudi-backed coalition to prove that his group of fighters didn't have any Al-Qaeda members. Slowly, and with the help of local tribal leaders, he succeeded in the following months.

At first the fighters sent me to their houses to stay with their wives, worried about a woman being near the front line. They made it clear to me that there were no journalists at their village so I insisted on leaving the house and they brought me by car to witness the fighting. At the front line, some of the fighters were wearing camouflage fatigues but they didn't have any combat helmets or vests. In typical Yemeni style, they were chewing qat to stay calm and concentrated. Another local leader was nicknamed Al-Britany (the Briton). Using a nom de guerre was standard practice by senior figures in the resistance against the Houthis because the rebel group controlled the main telecoms companies in Yemen and could tap phone calls easily.

Al Bayda's topography meant that the frontlines were on hillsides and the local defenders pointed out where the Houthis were stationed on the high ground opposite them. There was a lull in the fighting, but the defenders fired some Kalashnikov rounds for reasons that remain unclear to me. The response from the Houthis was immediate; a tank shell, which luckily went over our heads without injuring anyone.

In the evening I stayed with 'Al-Britany's' family; his mother suffers from eczema brought on by the psychological pressure from her concern for her son and the proximity of the battlefront which was just a few steps away from her home. The family's children had stopped going to school. I discovered that most of the local schools had closed: in the region, the absence of Houthi control meant that salaries for teachers couldn't be distributed regularly, despite irregular funding arriving from expatriates. Additionally, the area remained devoid of international aid agencies, leaving it overlooked by the United Nations.

A couple of days later I returned to Aden and the Al Bayda activist who had arranged for me to visit the front line then connected me to some of Al Bayda's tribal sheikhs, a group of elderly men who direct the fighting from outside of the province. The sheikhs were aligned with the national government in the fight against the Houthis but at that time they were still not receiving much help from the coalition. One evening during Ramadan I chewed qat with them after they had broken their fast and listened to their stories. One of the sheiks told me that the pattern of violence and revenge in the governate has its roots in history, resurfacing again during the civil war of the 1960s, when the Al Bayda tribes fought alongside the Yemeni government, and the Nasserists, against the Zaydis.

 The Sheik also said that 'the money the Saudi-led coalition spent on the war in Yemen and financing the armed groups and militias, could have freed Yemen from the Houthis many times around.' This was in 2018 and despite the coalition continuing to pour money into the conflict little has changed since.

On my return to Egypt, I visited some of the injured Al Bayda fighters. I met a group of four, living in a cramped flat in a rundown area of Cairo. They were receiving medical care paid for by Yemeni expats. I wanted just to chat and offer any help if possible. They all had severe injuries in their hands, arms and legs. I asked a boy who hadn't yet turned 16, if he would like to resume his education when he recovers. He replied he wanted to

study war so he could continue fighting. It reminded me what Omar, the 30-something military leader had told me: when the civil war is finished, an even bigger conflict will start — a war of tribal revenge.

Almost a year later I heard from Al-Britany's family; the Houthis had completely captured Al Bayda. The fighters who survived had fled the province and went to another city in the south, or to Marib, to continue their struggle.

Right: A fighter chews qat and takes a rest between fighting in his base in Al Bayda.

A fighter in Al Bayda carries bread, baked by his wife, for breakfast with comrades ahead of combat.

Pro-government fighters at the front lines in Al Bayda take aim and fire at Houthi positions.

Pro-government fighters seen near a front line position in Al Bayda.

Abyan: The Centre of Al-Qaeda

The beginning of the emergence of the extremist Islamic group in Yemen started with the return of the Mujahideen in Afghanistan and their use against the socialist party that was ruling the south before and during the 1994 war. The Mujahideen were poured into Abyan and the neighbouring majority Sunni governorates of Al Bayda and Shabwa. But Abyan is most known as the centre of Al-Qaeda in Yemen.

As well as the original Al-Qaeda insurgency, there are two other formations of Al-Qaeda groups that have been used in Yemen by the former-president Ali Saleh and his foe Al-Ahmer to defeat their enemies.

I passed by Abyan in 2021 after a Yemeni friend introduced me to a lawyer from Ja'ar (the capital of Khanfir District in Abyan south-western Yemen). The lawyer told me before I went to make sure when I took public transportation from Aden to cover my face in the traditional Yemeni style for women. He picked me up from the bus stop.

I had a car ride with the lawyer and his friend. We went through Zinjibar (the regional capital of Abyan). He asked me to warn him before I took a photo from his car. The main towns there of Zinjibar and Ja'ar were seriously crippled by complex fighting in the last few years. You could easily see how people in Abyan pay a heavy price because their province was chosen as a base for Al-Qaeda members.

In 2011, Al-Qaeda took over the city entirely during the uprising against the former-president. The lawyer showed me a mosque that was once a cinema before

Al-Qaeda turned it into a base and a mosque for them (because for them watching movies is forbidden). In 2017, the UAE-backed Southern Forces were fighting with Al-Qaeda in Abyan, damaging part of the government building, which only has a small part in use by the Security Belt Forces. The clashes have pushed Al-Qaeda-linked militants into the Mihfid and Maraqsha mountains. The lawyer explained that they are still there behind the mountain areas we saw on our tour from a distance.

On the way, we also passed by many of the 'Security Belt Forces' which the UAE has funded and trained to be under the STC with their Southern flag, the emblem of the south which wants to separate from the north. Security Belt Forces also took over main government and army areas and set them up as bases. But as we passed the outskirts, the lawyer pointed to a mountain area. 'Behind this area there're forces still loyal to the president (internationally recognised government supported by the Islah party) opposing the Security Belt Forces,' he said. Further behind this area we came close to in the Marashqa mountains, which the lawyer said were Al-Qaeda strongholds.

He also said that some of Al-Qaeda forces work with both sides. 'What is ridiculous is that they all buy qat from the same qat market [without hostility]. But this still makes people avoid this market because a bullet can be shot at any time,' he said.

I was told Al-Qaeda has been gaining strength in Abyan since 2015 since its militants have been fighting against

the Houthis in some parts of Yemen. This has reinforced their status within the tribes who want to fight Houthis and have been previously trying to fight against Al-Qaeda's expansion.

In-spite of the US attacks against Al-Qaeda, residents say the terrorist group was only pushed away to the mountains 'but they haven't changed their tactics.'

The lawyer said that for many southerners, the unification of Yemen during the regime of the autocratic Abdullah Saleh, who was denounced and rejected during the Arab Spring, was an unequal one. Southerners say the unification ended in 1994, after which they called it occupation, war, and marginalisation of the southern leaders. 'If it's up to me, I don't prefer secession,' the lawyer told me. 'But I want a unity where my son and grandson have stability, I want a unity based on equality. The northern Zaydi tribes have ruled for one thousand years and they still want to be ruling forever, they need to be aware of the tribal sensitivities, after all, and the previous wars and the multi political parties who need to share power.'

Shabwa: Tribes and Business

The importance of the Shabwa governate lies in its natural resources of gas and oil. It has two strategic ports for the export of hydrocarbons including a 320km gas pipeline running east to west to the port of Belhaf that exports liquefied gas. The Belhaf gas project is the biggest in the country with an international investment of $6 billion. But it has stopped production completely following the Arab Spring in 2011 and its aftermath. The French Total company owns most of the shares.

Because of its proximity to Al Bayda and Abyan, Al-Qaeda is present in some parts at the outskirts of Shabwa near Abyan. Unlike Al Bayda, which has some Zaydi tribes close to the north, Shabwa, is characterised by its powerful Sunni tribes who are big supporters of the Islah party.

Shabwa doesn't have a popular base for the Zaydis except for this part in the eastern area of 'Baiyhan' where some villages with Zaydi origins sympathise with the Houthis.

All of the above made Shabwa an open battlefield during the civil war. It was governed by different forces from 2015 to 2021. First the Houthis took over, then the legitimate government with the Islah party, then the UAE-backed elite forces and the STC before later falling again under the control of Islah then the STC and the coalition.

When I went to Shabwa in early 2020, the STC and the elite forces formed by the Emirates were in control of the city after some clashes with Islah forces. The Southern flag was drawn on street walls around Ataq, the capital.

Pictures of the UAE princes were drawn in a few places but the governor of Shabwa was pro the internationally-recognised government's forces.

For the STC, Shabwa secures their control over Abyan and other governates such as Aden, Al-Dhalea and Lahj. A few months before I arrived, Aden witnessed bloody clashes between the Security Belt Forces and the legitimate forces, the former took control of the city. Shabwa witnessed some clashes as well but government forces were still in control when I arrived.

I interviewed the governor of Shabwa while there, 'The UAE is using the Belhaf facility as a military base and a detention centre,' said Shabwa's governor, Muhammad Salih Ibn Adiu, 'No one is allowed to enter even to ask about their detained relatives or know their whereabouts or to visit them.' According to Riyadh's agreement, and after the government regained control over Shabwa, the UAE was supposed to leave Belhaf 'but they delayed in order to gain time so they can use the airports and the ports to distribute weapons for the militias they're backing.'

An Associated Press investigation by Maggie Michael (who wrote the foreword for this book) in 2018 found a network of secret prisons that was run either directly by the UAE or through allies. The investigation included interviews with former inmates and security officials who reported seeing Emirati officials at the facilities, where they also said the inmates were often tortured. Both Human Rights Watch and the UN confirmed the existence of Emirati-controlled prisons and torture

Adiu also said that 'the Emirates is backing other militias to weaken the internationally-approved government, claiming it is fighting Al-Qaeda while using some hardliners of Al-Qaeda in its elite forces.'

The UAE set up Shabwa Elite Forces in Shabwa which are made up of some factions of the southern movement and some opponents of the president. The Security Belt Forces in Shabwa have changed their name to Shabwa Defence Forces now. The soldiers make 10 times the salary of the government forces, so sometimes they register for both.

More than that, the Al-Qaeda presence in some areas in Shabwa made it an open war with the elite and coalition forces. But the legitimate forces are weak compared to the elite forces who have heavy military equipment. Until this year, the UAE are still present on the ground with forces in Belhaf and the Morra military base, close to Ataq, with more than 20 UAE officers. The defence elite forces facilitate the crossing of UAE forces from Belhaf to Ataq. Although the UAE handed over some authorities to Saudi Arabia, in reality all ports are controlled by the UAE with the elite forces they back.

In 2022, clashes occurred between elite forces and the legitimate pro-government forces when the legitimate forces stopped UAE-backed forces inspecting a military convoy. The UAE complained to Saudi Arabia, who appointed another governor than Adiu. According to a human rights activist in Shabwa, there are many people still detained as Al-Qaeda suspects.

Above, right: Workers manufacturing traditional janbiya daggers in Shabwa.

Left: Men walk past a painting on the wall of a building in Shabwa of (from left to right) Mohammed bin Rashid, the current ruler of Dubai, Khalifa bin Zayed, former president of the UAE, and Mohamed bin Zayed, current president of the UAE.

A maintenance shop in Shabwa where workers fix and tune up weapons.

Hadramout: The Lone Wolf

Hadramout is the historical province that embraced one of the oldest and most important kingdoms in history. The Hadramout Governorate is located in the east of Yemen and occupies 36 percent of its area. Unlike many major provinces in Yemen, the Houthis were not able to reach the Hadramout Governorate when they started to expand into the provinces after taking control of the country. The capital, Al Mukalla, has one of the main airports in Yemen, where it was under UAE control, and has just recently been opened again after many years when it was replaced for passengers by the small airport in Seiyun city.

Hadramout is a large oil producer in Yemen. It's also famous for producing honey in the Dawan area and Shibam town, known for its tall mud brick buildings and is referred to as the 'Manhattan of the Desert.'

People from Hadramout see themselves as part of a very independent region. They support federalism in the governorates of Mahra and Socotra at the east end of the country. The province is well known for its merchants and for the historical heritage that used to attract tourism before the civil war. The first popular southern movement against the north rose up in Hadramout and at first, it was a peaceful one. People in Hadramout don't use weapons, or wear daggers and so they're far removed from the gun culture. They also have a different accent compared to other nearby provinces. The UAE and its STC proxy, formed the Hadramout Elite Force – one of the many militias that the UAE formed – made up of the sons of the province. After long-term negotiations with their delegations in Saudi Arabia, they recently managed to form an autonomous region. A large population from Hadramout resides in Saudi Arabia and so they have very strong ties there.

A view of the historic Alguwizi fortress in Al Mukalla City, capital of Hadramout.

A view of the historic city of
Al Hajarayn in Hadramout.

A view of Shibam town in Hadramout known for its high buildings made from mud bricks and referred to as the 'Manhattan of the Desert.'

Children play football in an open area next to traditional buildings in Wadi Dawan, Hadramout.

Whither Yemen?

The situation is very complicated in Yemen. According to some analyses, the Houthis are actually establishing the Imamate now. They are winning and their rivals are losing. According to Maysaa Shuja Al-Deen, senior researcher at Sana'a Center for Strategic Studies, 'as militias, Houthis are winning because they managed to survive and they can expand militarily, although it is difficult for them to control more areas than they did. They now have a de facto quasi-state in which they implement their theocratic perceptions of governance.'

The Saudis were forced into a near pullout and halt of the war after Houthis waged attacks against Saudi oil installations. To defuse the Houthi threat, the Saudis rushed to seal a deal with both Iran and the Houthis. Now the Houthis are no longer targeting Saudi Arabia, and they have become the uncontested rulers of most of Yemen: 70 percent of the population live in Houthi-controlled areas.

Maysaa Shuja Al-Deen comments 'Since the coalition forces were stopped from advancing on the western coast according to the Stockholm Agreement in 2018, they were no longer able to expand and the UAE withdrew. Then Saudi Arabia adopted a defensive posture as a result of the Houthi attack on Marib, which was the largest and bloodiest battle in the Yemeni war and continued. Even the Houthis failed to seize the wealthy part of Marib, so both sides arguably felt unable to expand militarily beyond what they had.'

The south is fragmented, the internationally recognised government is extremely weak and rules parts of the

south from locations in Riyadh and Cairo, and the Yemeni ministers stay in Saudi Arabia or Egypt. The UAE established secessionist militias in the south. The future of southern Yemen is bleak. Tariq's forces control a large part of the north with their officers stationed in Mocha. Marib is under the Islah group. The south is divided: Aden, Abyan and Al-Dhalea are under the Southern Transitional Council and most of Shabwa as well. Even Hadramout is fragmented between the Saudi-backed coast and the UAE-controlled valleys.

Nine years on, the coalition hasn't reached Hodeidah, but rather retreated by 100 kilometres to the south. The Houthis didn't manage to take Marib although they came close. The civil war has destroyed a large part of the country's infrastructure and killed thousands of civilians. The country is still divided and millions of displaced people are still far from their homes.

The Houthis are gaining more power because Saudis are striking a deal with them, giving them legitimacy and declaring that they have lost the war. They are also gaining power because of the weakness of their rivals in addition to Iran's support. The civil war made Yemen the world's worst humanitarian crisis. For the Yemenis, the parties involved in the conflict continue to exploit international support and humanitarian aid for their personal gain.

A much-coveted truce, signed on 2 April 2022, now hangs in the balance as regional geopolitics take a turn for the worse. Israel's unyielding war on Gaza following attacks by Hamas on 7 October 2023 has raised an

outcry internationally. The Houthis – Ansar Allah – entered the fray by disrupting global shipping through the Red Sea in a show of solidarity with Palestine, triggering US and British airstrikes in return. The Houthis are exploiting the war to market themselves as the defenders of Islam while acting like pirates. Many see that the main gain from the attacks is that Iran has proved that it can cripple international shipping and trade by using the Houthis when they choose to.

Again, Maysaa Shuja Al-Deen offers valuable commentary 'the Houthis are a group that has ambitions to play a regional role and its ambitions since the beginning of its inception have gone beyond Yemen, and this is present in their literature. After the Hamas attack in October, Abdul-Malik al-Houthi stated that they are coordinating with the axis of resistance on how to respond and made it clear that it will be gradual. Saudi Arabia did not intervene because, like the rest of the Arab countries (with the exception of Bahrain), they felt that these strikes would appear to be support for Israel and the priority was to stop the Israeli aggression on Gaza, and also because it wanted to neutralise itself from the current conflict for economic and security reasons, and its calculations may change after the Gaza war, and it then depends on the development of events.'

As the Americans initiated attacks on the Houthis in response to their assault on shipping, the Saudis maintained silence. Any endeavor to remove the Houthis necessitates Saudi participation, which appears unlikely as long as the Houthis pose a threat to the Saudi economy. Given Saudi Arabia's crucial role in the global oil market, the Houthis not only wield control over the Red Sea but also effectively hold Saudi oil captive.

Meanwhile in Yemen, the long-awaited peace agreement sits idle in the midst of the new chaos engulfing the Middle East. Since 2022, all Yemeni political groups and entities have held fast to the truce under the auspices of the United Nations between the Yemeni government and the Houthis. The truce, which had been renewed almost three times along with negotiations for a ceasefire, remains elusive.

For many Yemenis, living under the Houthis is a nightmare. The reality is that any peace deal will be temporary until there is a united front that is strong enough to dislodge the Houthis. How will the Houthis govern the areas under their control? Will there ever be elections? Is there a normal constitution? Parliament? Political parties? There has not been any normal political structure to replace Ali Abdullah Saleh's state. Just some men from one family and their loyalists ruling with weapons.

Even if the war ends, the effects of the conflict will remain for many years to come. The list of what needs to happen to achieve peace and stability is long. The reunification of the state; the dissolution of military formations, and what seems most complicated: the south with its separate competing forces. Then there is Hadramout, which wants to secede and has its separate military formations (the Hadrami Elite Forces). Then there is Aidarous and the separatists who aspire

to control the entire south. The UAE and Saudis are in competition to control parts of Yemen.

Most Yemenis I met are aware of the effects of the proxy war in Yemen. A displaced woman from Hodeidah that I keep in touch with, who is still displaced in Al-Khokha town, told me that Yemenis were happy at first when the coalition offered them weapons and training, denied by the former-president because he had favoured those tribes in power. 'But now for many years we're still not in our homes,' she said, 'but it would have been better if they had just left us Yemenis to fight each other on our own. We have strong men and we would have finished the fighting a long time ago.'

Right: Women farmers harvest vegetables from a field at the foot of the mountains in Wadi Dawan, Hadramout.

Asmaa Waguih is an independent photojournalist based in her hometown of Cairo. She has over two decades of experience working with top agencies across the globe. She worked for Reuters News Agency for eight years covering many conflicts including Iraq and Afghanistan. She has been travelling to Yemen on a regular basis since 2016 to document the ongoing conflict.